Ripley's Believe It or Not!®

Developed and produced by Ripley Publishing Ltd

This edition published and distributed by:

Mason Crest
370 Reed Road, Broomall, Pennsylvania 19008
www.masoncrest.com

Printed and bound in the United States of America.

First printing
9 8 7 6 5 4 3 2 1

Ripley's Believe It or Not!
Strange Tales
ISBN-13: 978-1-4222-2575-2 (hardcover)
ISBN-13: 978-1-4222-9250-1 (e-book)
Ripley's Believe It or Not!–Complete 16 Title Series
ISBN-13: 978-1-4222-2560-8

Library of Congress Cataloging-in-Publication Data

Strange tales.
    p. cm. – (Ripley's believe it or not!)
  ISBN 978-1-4222-2575-2 (hardcover) – ISBN 978-1-4222-2560-8 (series hardcover) –
ISBN 978-1-4222-9250-1 (ebook)
  1. Tales.
  GR76.P74 2012
  398.2–dc23
                        2012020382

PUBLISHER'S NOTE
While every effort has been made to verify the accuracy of the entries in this book, the Publisher's cannot be held responsible for any errors contained in the work. They would be glad to receive any information from readers.

WARNING
Some of the stunts and activities in this book are undertaken by experts and should not be attempted by anyone without adequate training and supervision.

Disbelief and Shock!

STRANGE TALES

www.MasonCrest.com

STRANGE TALES

Wacky world. Find a host of incredible performers,

freaky foods, and remarkable stories when you

delve inside this book. Read about the man who

juggles live chainsaws, the 20-ft-wide (6-m) mega

donut made from 90,000 ring donuts, and the

snake that swallowed golf balls!

*This dress in Mumbai, India, is big enough to
fit more than a dozen ordinary-sized women.*

THE BOY
BEHIND THE MASK

Little Joshua Taylor's family never know what he is going to look like from one minute to the next—because he has a collection of more than 400 masks.

Six-year-old Joshua from West Jefferson, North Carolina, has been fascinated by masks since he was 18 months old, when he watched the movie *The Haunted Mask* at every available opportunity. He started wearing a werewolf mask wherever he went before progressing to making his own masks... from food.

He would bite out eyes, nose, and mouth from bologna (sliced sausage) and even designed a mask from a tortilla. His mom Angie says: "He chewed out a face from the tortilla and put it in the refrigerator for days, and it had an old wooden look to it. It amazes me to watch his creativity."

Joshua has also made masks from papier mâché and for Christmas 2006 was given his first rubber-mask-making kit. Now the talented youngster is able to devise an amazing range of latex masks—from the grotesque to the humorous.

Angie Taylor says: "He is fascinated with facial features, noses, cheeks, and shapes and we have started to look at it as an art form. We plan on making him an area in the basement to be his workshop where he can build, create, and sculpt all he wants."

Young Joshua Taylor has more than 400 masks, many of which he has made himself. A variety of monsters, aliens, superheroes, and skeletons feature in his extensive collection.

PARALLEL BIRTHS

Identical twins Nicole Cramer and Naomi Sale of Auburn, Indiana, both gave birth to a son at the same hospital on the same day—January 23, 2007.

LUCKY OMEN

After getting married on a Lake Michigan beach on August 18, 2007, Melody Kloska and Matt Behrs released a bottle containing their wedding vows. A few weeks later, it was picked up by Fred and Lynnette Dubendorf, of Mears, Michigan, who were also married on a beach—28 years to the day before Kloska and Behrs.

WAD A FIND!

In 2007, British archeology student Sarah Pickin discovered a 5,000-year-old piece of chewing gum at a dig site in western Finland.

CANNED FISH

A fish caught off the coast of Iceland in 2007 was wearing a tin can that had grown into its flesh. The fish must have looked into the can and become partly trapped. When fishermen first spotted the halibut, they thought it was wearing tribal jewelry.

SQUIRREL FIND

Squirrels in Placer County, California, dug up an ancient artifact in July 2007. The animals were rummaging around in soil at the Maidu Indian Interpretive Center—where it is illegal for human archeologists to dig—when they unearthed a 10,000-year-old carved tool.

JACKPOT JOY

After winning $10,000 on the Arizona Lottery in 2007, Barbara and Barry Salzman of Henderson, Nevada, immediately bought another ticket with their winnings and won the $15-million jackpot.

HIDDEN WINNINGS

In 2007, demolition workers at the Sands Casino in Atlantic City, New Jersey, discovered a staggering $17,193.34 in tokens, coins, and bills that had fallen underneath the slot machines.

HEADLESS CORPSES

Archeologists on the Pacific island of Vanuatu recently discovered a 3,000-year-old cemetery in which every single body they found had been decapitated.

IN A SPIN

Eight-year-old Patrick Grieves of Essex, England, accepted a dare from his sister to climb into the family's washing machine—and ended up having to be rescued by ten firefighters after becoming wedged fast in the drum.

VIKING SHIP

Professor Steven Harding of the University of Nottingham, England, found a 1,000-year-old Viking ship buried under the parking lot of a pub in Merseyside.

LONG GONE

In October 2006, authorities in Vienna, Austria, discovered the mummified body of Franz Riedl who had been lying dead in his bed for at least five years.

LOST ARMY

In March 2007, some 170 Swiss soldiers got lost and accidentally invaded Liechtenstein, a defenseless country of only 34,000 people.

FEUDING BROTHERS

Two brothers have divided the house that they share with barbed wire because they keep fighting. Taso Hadjiev and his brother Asen from Malka Arda, Bulgaria, have sued each other more than 200 times over the past 40 years but neither can afford to leave the family home—because all their money has been spent on lawyers' fees.

WRAPPED UP

A Kenyan air passenger flying home from China in 2007 was found to be wearing more than 100 items of men's and women's clothing! He told officials that he had been worried about being charged for carrying excess luggage.

SHELL SHOCK

An elderly lady in England used a live German World War I artillery shell, which could have exploded at any time, as a doorstop for 20 years. The 7-in-long (18-cm) device had been collected by Thelma Bonnett's grandfather in 1918 while he served with the Merchant Navy. Thelma had used it as an ornament for decades in her home in Paignton, Devon. However, a neighbor sounded the alarm in 2007, after which bomb-disposal experts were called in to the home to deal with the shell, which was packed with explosives and had its mechanism primed to fire.

GROUNDHOG DAY

A woman from Ohio has given birth to three children on the same date in different years—odds of more than 130,000 to one. Jenna Cotton of Marysville gave birth to sons Ayden and Logan in 2003 and 2006 respectively, followed by daughter Kayla in 2007—all on October 2.

SOLDIERS REBURIED

On November 25, 2007, historical re-enactors dressed up as Napoleonic soldiers and helped to rebury the bodies of 223 French servicemen of the Grande Armée who had died in 1812 near the town of Studenka, Belarus, during Napoleon's invasion.

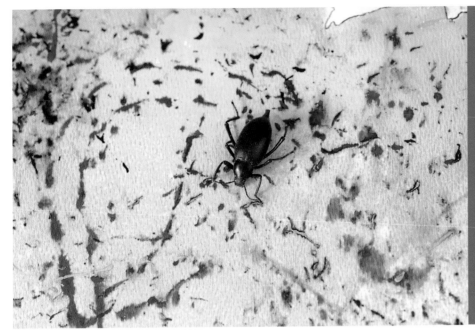

BUG ART

Los Angeles artist Steven Kutcher uses insects as living paintbrushes. He takes flies, cockroaches, and beetles in his hand and adds paint onto each leg, one leg at a time. He then releases them onto a prepared canvas, allowing them to create a trail of color. To ensure his insects come to no harm, he always uses water-based, nontoxic paints that wash off easily.

SKELETON IN LOFT

A man's skeleton was discovered in the loft of his family home in Bergholz-Rehbrücke, Germany, in 2007—22 years after his disappearance.

METAL ADDICT

The Swedish Employment Service granted disability payments to Roger Tullgren of Hassleholm, Sweden, because he is addicted to heavy-metal music. A heavy-metal fan since hearing Black Sabbath at the age of six, Tullgren attended 300 concerts in 2006, often skipping work to do so.

BODY FOUND

While researching a story in August 2007, Seattle-based author Peter Stekel discovered the frozen body of a World War II aviator on a Californian glacier.

CYANIDE TERROR

Nine villagers from Yangping, Henan, China, were killed in September 2007 when a floor collapsed and dumped them into an underground pool of cyanide that no one had known was there.

HARDENED CRIMINAL

Following an attempted carjack, police easily captured the fleeing suspect in Reno, Nevada, in November 2007, after he got stuck in wet concrete as he tried to make his escape through a construction site.

WALLET RECOVERED

A man who lost his wallet on a trip to the theater in 1964 got it back 43 years later. Construction workers renovating the Crest Theater at El Centro, California, discovered Epigmenio Sanchez's wallet jammed between the metal casings of a radiator.

DOUBLE BLOW

A man in Australia was attacked by a crocodile and then accidentally shot by his rescuer. Jason Grant had been collecting crocodile eggs at a reptile farm near Darwin when the saltwater croc seized him in his jaws. His colleague fired two shots at the crocodile and one struck Grant in the arm.

SNAKE'S TEE

When a python was taken to a wildlife sanctuary near Brisbane, Australia, with four bumps in its belly, veterinarians were amazed to see four golf balls show up on an X ray. The snake had swallowed the balls after apparently mistaking them for chicken eggs. Unable to pass the golf balls naturally, the snake underwent a successful operation to remove them and was later released back into the wild.

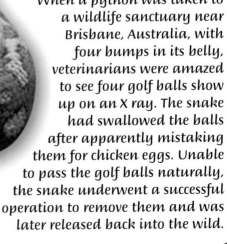

BE OUR GUEST

When comedian and filmmaker Mark Malkoff's New York City apartment had to be fumigated in January 2008, he obtained permission to move into an IKEA store for a week.

Reasoning that hotels were too expensive, he lived, slept, and ate at the store in Paramus, New Jersey. Malkoff took full advantage of the free accommodation and fully furnished rooms at the IKEA store. He said the only problems were that the display sinks and toilets were not plumbed in (forcing him to shower in the staff locker room) and at night the lights in the store automatically came on at 2 a.m. Although his wife chose not to join him on his IKEA holiday, Malkoff had numerous visitors to his temporary in-store living quarters and even staged a housewarming party.

Mark sorts through his underwear drawer in one of the bedrooms.

Breakfast in Mark's IKEA pad was a relaxed affair.

Mark in his IKEA bedroom...

kitchen...

and bathroom.

BITE SIZE

Sid the grass snake looked to have bitten off more than he could chew when tackling a goldfish more than ten times the size of his head at a garden in Kent, England. However, by dislocating his jaw he was eventually able to devour the tasty meal and continue his campaign to snatch fish up to 8 in (20 cm) long from the pond.

ANCIENT TOOTH

Researchers in Spain have unearthed a human tooth that is more than one million years old. The fossil was discovered near Burgos and sets a new date for humankind's presence in western Europe—the previous oldest finds for the region being a mere 800,000 years old!

STONE RIDDLE

In September 2007, residents in northern England and in Scotland were puzzled to find strange stone heads left outside their homes in the dead of night. More than 50 gargoyle-like figures were deposited throughout a wide area, each bearing a carving that spelled out the word "paradox." A riddle was also attached. The culprit turned out to be eccentric artist Billy Johnson, who had hoped the recipients would use the cryptic clues to contact his website.

GIANT PENGUIN

Scientists have discovered fossilized remains of a sun-loving giant penguin that lived some 36 million years ago and, at 5 ft (1.5 m), was as tall as an adult human. The skeleton was discovered on the southern coast of Peru, indicating that it preferred the tropics to colder climes.

RING RETURNED

Clare Cavoli Lopez of South Euclid, Ohio, lost her class ring while scuba diving off the coast of South Africa more than 20 years ago. Her ring was found in 2007 by a professional diver in an underwater cave on Mauritius and returned to her.

MISTAKEN IDENTITY

Bones long thought to belong to Joan of Arc were recently discovered to be those of an ancient Egyptian mummy and its pet cat.

FISH CURE

British scientists believe that a tiny tropical fish could help find a cure for blindness in humans. The zebrafish has a unique ability to repair its own damaged and diseased eyes, and now researchers have identified that the special cells, which restore sight in zebrafish, can also be found in the human eye.

CHILI LOVERS

Across the Americas, people were eating chili peppers as long as 6,000 years ago. Recent discoveries from the Bahamas to Peru found starch microfossils of grains from chili peppers alongside remnants of corn, yucca, squash, beans, and palm fruit, suggesting that the ancients used recipes that aimed to make bland tastes more palatable.

DUNG DEAL

While examining two mountain plateaus in southern Suriname in 2005, mining company researchers discovered 24 new species of animals—half of which were dung beetles.

ALL THE EIGHTS

In 2007, a baby was born in Liverpool, England, at eight minutes past eight in the morning of the eighth day of the eighth month weighing eight pounds, and after her mother had been in labor for eight hours! The mother, Mel Byrne, was looked after by a midwife who delivered eight babies that day.

TRIPLE CELEBRATION

The golf-crazy Mackenzie family beat odds of 15 million-to-one to score three holes-in-one in the space of three days in 2007. Dad Ray, wife Gill, and their 14-year-old son Sam all landed aces at the Llanfairfechan Golf Club in North Wales.

AGED CLAM

A quahog clam estimated to be more than 400 years old was found in the waters off Iceland in 2006—which means that when it was young, William Shakespeare was writing his greatest plays!

FAT FEAST

Croatian conceptual artist Zoran Todorovic fed human fat and skin from liposuction clinics to visitors to his exhibition in Zagreb.

SICK REMEDY

In April 2004, a Chinese man was arrested on suspicion of stealing 30 corpses from graveyards, cooking soup from their flesh, and crushing the bones in an attempt to heal his sick wife.

PRESERVED FROG

A frog was found inside a chunk of amber in Chiapas, Mexico—where it has been preserved for as long as 25 million years.

SOMETHING FISHY

In January 2007, customs officials in Thailand found more than 1,400 turtles of various species and 33 arapaima fish being smuggled out of the country in a single suitcase.

MAN-MADE TORNADO

A museum in Stuttgart, Germany, has created its own 113-ft-high (34.4-m) tornado. In order to remove smoke from the building in the event of a fire, the Mercedes-Benz Museum has devised a system that uses 144 air jets to form a powerful tornado from 28 tons of air.

WATCH RETURNED

A World War I veteran's engraved watch was returned to the owner's family in 2007—nearly 90 years after William B. Gill lost it in France, where he served in the U.S. Army. It was later won in a poker game and then, with the help of a genealogist, returned to Gill's grandchildren in Sioux City, Iowa.

BLOOD BROTHERS

A bull that broke loose gored two American brothers—Lawrence and Michael Lenahan—simultaneously, catching one on each of its horns during the 2007 Running of the Bulls Festival at Pamplona, Spain.

BOWLING ALLEY

Italian archeologists working in Egypt have found an indoor bowling alley that is nearly 2,000 years old. A large room, with a shallow lane running into a pit and two heavy stone balls lying nearby, was found at an ancient site that lies 55 mi (88 km) south of the Egyptian capital, Cairo.

SEVENTH HEAVEN

Herbethe Elie of Birmingham, England, gave birth to her seventh baby in the seventh hour of the seventh day of the seventh month of 2007—in hospital delivery room number seven.

GREAT SURVIVOR

A 50-ton bowhead whale caught off the coast of Alaska in 2007 had a weapon fragment embedded in its neck that showed it had survived a previous attack over a century before. The 3.5-in (9-cm), arrow-shaped projectile, thought to date from around 1890, was found deep under the whale's blubber.

NEIGHBORLY ACT

After two days adrift in the Caribbean, John Fildes was rescued by a cruise ship, which, amazingly, was captained by a neighbor from his hometown—Warsash, England.

CAR KISSING

A Chinese woman won a car in 2007 by kissing it virtually nonstop for more than 24 hours. Zhang Cunying was one of 120 people taking part in the endurance contest at a Beijing shopping mall, where the competitors had to kiss Chevrolet cars through plastic nipples attached to the bodywork but without touching the car itself. The person lasting the longest was declared the winner. They were allowed a ten-minute break every seven hours and, in order to speed up elimination, were eventually made to stand on one foot with their hands behind their back. Zhang owed her success to her dance training, although she was so exhausted at the finish that she could not stand up unaided.

HARRY'S HAT

Three-year-old Charlie Thomas from Cullompton, Devon, England, thought it would be a bright idea to put a traffic cone on his head so that he could look just like his hero, boy wizard Harry Potter... but when the cone stuck fast, he had to be cut free by six firefighters. After soap and tugging failed to remove the cone, the fire crews had to use cutting tools and pliers in a delicate half-hour operation.

HOTEL FALL

Joshua Hanson, of Wisconsin, plummeted 16 floors after falling through the window of a Minneapolis hotel in 2007, but survived because he landed on the roof overhang one floor up from the street.

UNUSUAL CASE

In 2007, a ten-year-old boy was hit by a car while walking to school in Lancaster, Pennsylvania, but escaped with only cuts and bruises because the violin case he was carrying took most of the impact.

BAD DAY

In 1945, Betty Lou Oliver of New York City survived a plane crash and a 1,000-ft (300-m) elevator fall on the same day.

DOUBLE STRIKE

Lightning can strike twice! On July 27, 2007, Don Frick of Hamlin, Pennsylvania, was at a festival when lightning struck the ground nearby, leaving a burned zipper and a hole in the back of his jeans—27 years to the day of his first strike. On July 27, 1980, he had been driving a tractor-trailer when the antenna was struck by lightning, injuring his left side.

BULL ATTACK

In 1912, 49-year-old "Granny" Anderson of Staples, Texas, had her intestines ripped out by a bull. A doctor washed the wound, replaced her innards, and sewed her up, and she went on to live to the age of 105.

UPSIDE DOWN

The pilot of a light airplane escaped injury in July 2007 when it landed on its roof at Darwin Airport, Australia. The plane was spun upside down by a fierce crosswind as it came in to land.

NAIL GUN

A three-month-old baby survived after being accidentally shot in the head by a nail gun. The boy was sitting on his mother's lap near a construction site in Delta, Colorado, when a nail fired from the gun ricocheted off boards and hit him in the head.

PLUGGED HOLE

Shot in the heart with a 3-in (7.6-cm) nail, 17-year-old Matt Robinson of Dexter, Missouri, survived the ordeal only because he didn't bleed. Miraculously, the nail plugged the hole it had made until a doctor could operate.

HANGING AROUND

An 85-year-old man fell from a fifth-floor window in Zhengzhou, China, in 2007—but was saved by a nail. The nail, located in the wall between the fourth and fifth floors, snagged Zhao Jinghzi's clothing and held his weight until help arrived.

GRASS DIET

Lost in the hot Canadian wilderness for nine days in July 2007, 78-year-old Norm Berg, of Alberta, survived by eating grass and leaves.

WHEELCHAIR RIDE

A wheelchair user was taken on a terrifying 50-mph (80-km/h) ride for 4 mi (6.4 km) along a U.S. highway in 2007 after his handlebars became wedged in the front grill of a truck.

Ben Carpenter, a 21-year-old man with muscular-dystrophy, was crossing the street in Paw Paw, Michigan, when the back of his motorized wheelchair was bumped by a truck leaving a gas station, the impact trapping the chair in the radiator grill. The truck driver then drove off down the highway, unaware that he had an involuntary passenger on the front of his vehicle.

Luckily, horrified passers-by saw Carpenter's predicament and alerted the police, who eventually managed to stop the truck. Carpenter was unhurt, having been held in place in his wheelchair by a seatbelt. Afterward he said: "It was quite a ride."

Incredibly, Ben Carpenter emerged unharmed from his high-speed ride... apart from losing his hat and spilling his soda.

The driver refused to believe there was a man stuck to the front of his truck... until he saw it for himself.

"It was pretty scary," said Ben Carpenter of his ordeal. "I tried to yell for help, but no one could hear me."

b A truck slowly pulls out of a gas station and hits Ben's wheelchair, which becomes attached to the front grill.

a Ben Carpenter crosses the road.

c Truck accelerates to 50 mph. Ben is carried along the highway.

d Passing vehicles call 911. Ben's chair is attached to the truck for 4 mi (6.4 km) before the police intervene.

SCORPION SKEWERS

Conveniently served on wooden skewers, fried scorpions and centipedes were two of the delicacies on offer at one of the food stalls at the Nanjing Food Fest in China.

SCORPION SCALOPPINE
Ingredients:

8 frozen desert hairy scorpions (*Hadrurus arizonensis*) or similar species, thawed

1 pint low-fat milk

1 cup white cornmeal

2 tablespoons unsalted butter

1 tablespoon fresh lemon juice

2 tablespoons fresh parsley, chopped

Using a sharp knife, remove and discard stingers and venom glands from the tips of the scorpions' tails.

Pour milk into a medium-sized bowl; add scorpions and set aside while preparing the rest of the ingredients.

In a 12-in (30-cm) skillet, melt the butter. Remove scorpions from the milk mixture, allowing excess to drain off. Dredge the scorpions through the cornmeal, one at a time. Shake off excess flour.

Place the scorpions in the hot butter and cook until golden brown (about 2 minutes), then turn scorpions over and cook until done (about 1 minute).

Drain on paper towels and sprinkle with lemon juice and chopped parsley.

The Eat-a-Bug Cookbook by David George Gordon, in which the above recipe appears, offers adventurous cooks "33 ways to cook grasshoppers, ants, water bugs, spiders, centipedes, and their kin."

THAT'S CRACKERS!

A factory in the Japanese town of Omachi is the proud producer of rice crackers that contain the added protein of digger wasps. The "jibachi senbei" or "digger wasp rice cracker" is a delicacy that has been specially commissioned by a Japanese fan club for wasps. Fan club members say that the extra ingredient adds a waspish note to the traditional flavor of the crackers.

SNAKE SNACK

Shyam Atulkar from Nagpur, India, catches snakes and sometimes eats them alive! "I like the taste of snakes," he says, "especially the tail end, which tastes like raw mutton. The head and neck taste somewhat bitter because of the poison."

COCKROACH CONTEST

With his hands tied behind his back, Shai Pariente ate 13 oven-cooked cockroaches in New York in 2004 to win an iPod in a contest.

ANT COOKIES

Cookies made with *bachaco*, a type of large ant, were served during a demonstration by Venezuelan chef Nelson Mendez at a food fair in Caracas in 2007.

SCORPION ADDICT

Hasip Kaya of Turkey has become addicted to eating live scorpions. The father-of-two has been eating them since childhood and enjoys them so much that villagers search under rocks to find him fresh supplies.

BEATING HEART

A delicacy in Japanese restaurants is the still beating heart of a freshly-killed frog! The dish is said to be particularly tasty if accompanied by lizard sake.

TASTY TARANTULA

A Cambodian woman munches on a tasty fried spider as she passes through the town of Skuon, which is also known as Spider Town to the locals. The spiders, which are collected from the surrounding countryside, are deep fried in salt and garlic. Customers wash the meal down with a bowl of medicinal tarantula wine, which is served with the rotting spiders' bodies still lying in the bottom of the bowl, with the fangs intact to prevent the medicine from losing its power.

RATTLESNAKE TACO

The Mexican town of Santiago de Anaya hosted a gastronomic festival featuring more than a thousand dishes made from all kinds of local flora and fauna in April 2007. This local resident is seen enjoying a taco made from rattlesnake meat.

FIRST AUCTION

A bottle of 81-year-old scotch was sold for $54,000 in 2007—in New York State's first liquor auction since Prohibition. Although Prohibition ended in 1933, the state continued to ban the auctioning of spirits until recently.

COFFEE GUM

People in Japan can buy coffee-flavored chewing gum that leaves their breath coffee-fresh.

INSECT TREAT

For centuries, farmers in Santander, Colombia, have harvested queen ants as a tasty treat for local consumption. They now export the ants abroad as gourmet delights.

CHEESE BRIBE

Four police officers in the Campagnia region of Italy were arrested in 2007 for demanding mozzarella bribes from motorists. They were said to have stopped cheese delivery trucks and forced the drivers to hand over the contents or face a large fine.

WORM MAN

Wayne Fauser, alias The Worm Man, from Sydney, Australia, eats live earthworms, either in sandwiches or just plain.

CHOCOLATE SIN

Two hundred years ago chocolate was considered to be a temptation of the devil. In some Central American mountain villages, no one under the age of 60 was allowed to taste it and churchgoers who defied the ruling were threatened with excommunication.

HOT STUFF

A two-year-old boy in Assam, India, has become addicted to Bhut Jolakia, the world's hottest chili. Young Jayanta Lahan has eagerly devoured the chilies ever since he first tried them while his mother was cooking when he was eight months old. He can eat about 50 of these chilies in three hours without suffering any ill effects—they are so hot that they would make most of us cry involuntarily and suffer a burning sensation in the stomach. The Bhut Jolokia is one hundred times hotter than a Jalapeno pepper and has half the potency of weapon-grade pepper spray!

Enter the Vault

◀ SHARP APPETITE

Professor Leo Kongee of Pittsburgh, Pennsylvania, ate with a hatpin stuck through his cheeks to prevent him from eating too fast!

PILES OF PASTA

A marathon spaghetti-eater works his way through mountains of pasta at Ripley's New York City Odditorium in 1939. Giuseppe Ricore ate a mammoth 1½ mi (2.4 km) of spaghetti in three hours.

SKINNY DINER

This slender eatery in 1940s Miami, Florida, was a mere 50 in (130 cm) wide. It stretched back 52 ft (16 m), however, so it could accommodate a long line of hungry diners.

BEER BONANZA

The strong, steady hands of Bavarian waiter Clemens Pichl could carry 35 beer steins, full of beer, at the same time in Old Heidelberg, Pittsford, New York in 1935.

COLOSSAL CAKE ▶

This giant wedding cake measured 15½ ft (4.7 m) tall, and was baked for the county fair in Ferndale, California, in the 1950s. The cake served no fewer than 10,500 people!

OYSTER LOVER

During the 1930s, Joseph A. Cohen of Douglas, Arizona, could eat 120 fried oysters at a single sitting, and did so on many occasions.

BIG BEAN

Backyard gardener C.W. Forschner of Cleveland, Ohio, grew a butter bean that measured 27½ in (70 cm) in length and 20½ in (52 cm) in diameter.

CORN-UCOPIA

Champion sweet-corn eater Ed Kottwitz of Ortonville, Minnesota, once ate 50 large ears of corn in one mammoth corn-eating session in the 1930s.

◀ BRAVE BAKER

In 1935, in a feat of finger-tingling dexterity, George Gotsis of Chicago, Illinois, cut a 16-in (40-cm) loaf of bread into perfect slices in 40 seconds, while wearing a blindfold!

PIE-MAKER ▶ EXTRAORDINAIRE

Mrs W. E. Updegraff of Vinita, Oklahoma, made 60 pies in just 45 minutes, every weekday for a period of no less than 23 years. During this time she baked more than an astonishing 380,000 pies!

Ripley's Believe It or Not!

DUCK OVERBOARD!

In January 1992, a stupendous storm washed three containers off a ship that was bound from Hong Kong to Tacoma, Washington. One container spilled its contents into the sea—no less than 29,000 bathtub toys!

Two-thirds of them bobbed off south through the tropics, landing months later on the shores of Indonesia, Australia, and South America. The remaining 10,000 plastic ducks, turtles, frogs, and beavers headed north and were soon off the coast of Alaska whereupon they turned back westward. Some of the ducks made their way south and were seen floating past Japan in 1995. Many, however, became trapped in the North Pacific Gyre. This giant clockwise spiral of water collects and gradually grinds the oceans' plastic debris. However, even this couldn't halt the plucky ducks, which eventually broke free and pressed on. They bravely steered a course for the Arctic where some became trapped in ice for several years.

They finally reached the North Atlantic in 2000 and, in the summer of 2007, more than 15 years and nearly 17,000 mi (27,500 km) after their journey's start, flotillas of ducks, bleached white by the sun and sea, hit the coasts of Great Britain and North America.

In 2007, retired teacher Penny Harris found the first plastic duck from the cargo to arrive in England when it washed up on a beach in Devon at the end of a 15-year round-the-world trip.

Global travels...

5 Between 1995 and 2000 ducks become trapped in slow-moving ice at the top of the world.

2 Ship hit in storm in January 1992; container is washed overboard spilling 29,000 plastic bath toys.

1 Ship leaves Hong Kong bound for U.S.A.

4 Many of the toys are caught in the North Pacific Gyre and float in a 6,800-mi (11,000-km) loop from 1992 to 1995.

6 In 2001 ducks are tracked in an area where the Titanic sank.

3 19,000 toys bob along southward and wash up on the shores of Australia, Indonesia, and South America.

7 After a 15-year journey, the ducks head south into the Atlantic and are caught in the Gulf Stream, which brings them bobbing toward the southwest coast of the U.K. in summer 2007.

SAME DATE

Lila Debry-Martin of Kingston Peninsula, New Brunswick, Canada, gave birth to triplets on August 10, 2000—the same day that she had given birth to twins three years before.

BIRTHDAY BONANZA

Michele Rosciano, his son Giovanni, and his grandson Miguel were all born as the second child, on the same day, of the same month, in the same hour—just in different years.

HOCKEY RING

A Stanley Cup hockey championship ring that had been missing for more than 30 years has been found in the Gulf of Mexico. It belonged to former Toronto Maple Leafs' player Jim Pappin who later gave it to his father-in-law when he was traded to the Chicago Blackhawks. The ring was lost near Vero Beach, Florida, in the 1970s, but in 2007, a treasure hunter with an underwater metal detector found it with Pappin's name inscribed on the inside.

ANCIENT MUSHROOM

U.S. scientists say that a mushroom found embedded in a piece of amber in Myanmar is 100 million years old—an age that makes it 20 million years older than any other known mushroom fossils.

GOLFING DOUBLE

Two members of a foursome scored back-to-back holes-in-one at a New Jersey golf club in 2007—defying odds of more than 17 million to one! Immediately after nine-handicapper Thomas Brady landed an ace at the 179-yd (164-m) seventh hole at Forsgate Country Club in Monroe Township, Dennis Gerhart, a self-confessed "weekend hacker" who plays golf only 15 times a year, stepped up to the tee and emulated the feat.

CHIP AND PIN

In February 2007, grandmother Olga Mauriello of San Giorgio Cremano, Italy, found a live World-War-II-era grenade—without its safety pin—in a sack of potatoes.

WHALE FOSSIL

In early 2007, paleontologists discovered a near-complete five-million-year-old whale fossil beneath a vineyard in Tuscany, Italy.

CLOSE RELATIVES

Unbeknown to each other, Dorothy Caudle lived just 300 ft (100 m) from her sister Gladys Clark for an entire year. The sisters, who had not seen each other for 38 years, were living in the same senior care facility at Tempe, Arizona, but did not realize it until celebrations were held to mark Clark's 100th birthday in 2007.

SURPRISE LEGACY

Men carrying out plumbing work on Mike Sutton's new house in Bridport, Dorset, England, took up the cellar floor and found hundreds of artificial legs!

PETRIFIED FOREST

A forest of around 200 petrified trees has been discovered in Washington State, still standing on the spot where they were swamped by lava more than 15 million years ago. Clyde Friend used an excavator, a hammer, and a chisel to unearth the forest of preserved hickory, maple, elm, and sweetgum trees on his land near Yakima.

FRESH FRUIT

Archeologists in western Japan have unearthed a 2,100-year-old melon—with its flesh still on the rind. They believe it had been preserved for centuries because it had been in a vacuum-packed state in a wet layer below the ground, where it was immune to attack from microorganisms.

EGG RETURNED

A rare bird's egg was returned to a museum in the town of Salcombe in Devon, England, in 2006—43 years after it had been stolen. The bustard's egg arrived back in mint condition, accompanied by a letter signed only "John," apologizing for the theft in 1963.

JAILHOUSE ROCK

Hundreds of inmates at the Cebu Detention and Rehabilitation Center in the Philippines re-created the famous video dance routine to Michael Jackson's "Thriller." Their version proved so popular that by the end of 2007 it had been viewed more than 10 million times on YouTube—twice as many as had watched Jackson's original! The routine was an exercise program devised by security consultant Byron Garcia. Dancing is compulsory for all 1,600 inmates (except the elderly and the infirm) at Cebu and two former prisoners there have even gone on to become professional dancers.

BUMPER CRIME

A white Ford Ranger pickup truck stolen in Miami, Florida, was recovered five days later. The only things missing were 700 bumper stickers that had been covering the exterior.

FAKE BILL

Police arrested a man after he handed over a fake million-dollar bill at a Pittsburgh, Pennsylvania, supermarket and asked for change. When staff refused and confiscated the note, the man became abusive.

JESUS IMAGE

A smudge of driveway sealant said to resemble the face of Jesus was sold for more than $1,500 in an online auction. The image was found on the garage floor of the Serio family home in the town of Forest, Virginia.

DOUBLE THEFT

York Heiden of Stevens Point, Wisconsin, had his car stolen twice in one day: April 27, 2007.

LUCKY NUMBER

A woman from Devon, England, won the equivalent of $2.6 million in the lottery because she forgot the age of her son. Janet Baddick chooses numbers representing family ages, but used 26 for her son Darren, forgetting that he had turned 27 a few weeks earlier. Luckily, 26 was a winning number!

FAMILY TIES

When an off-duty jail deputy in Nevada was pulled over and charged with driving under the influence, the arresting officer was her husband. Charlotte Moore was driving her 2004 Pontiac when she was stopped by husband Mike, a deputy with the Elko County Sheriff's Department.

BOX WARS

In a craze that started in Melbourne, Australia, people fight battles wearing suits of armor made of cardboard. The rules of Box Wars—which has spread to Canada, the United States, and Britain—state that only cardboard, tape, and spray paint may be used for armor and weapons. Battles last around 15 minutes each and end when no one is left wearing any cardboard.

LOVE MOTIVE

Police in Inglewood, California, arrested a man in April 2007 for stealing 26 cars that he used only to visit his girlfriend.

LUCKY MISTAKE

Derek Ladner of Cornwall, England, accidentally bought two lottery tickets with the same sequence of numbers. The numbers came up, meaning that he won a share of the jackpot—the equivalent of nearly $1 million—twice over!

LOOK, NO ARMS!

A driver in Pasco County, Florida, lost police in an 8-minute high-speed car chase in 2007 despite having no arms and only one leg. Officers said that 40-year-old Michael Wiley, who had had been sighted out in his car while legally suspended from driving, had overcome three amputations and had learned to drive with his stumps. In 1998, Wiley had also caused a highway car chase that reached speeds of 120 mph (193 km/h).

BRIDGE STOLEN

In August 2007, police in Ryazan, Russia, arrested a man for stealing an entire 16-ft-long (5-m) steel bridge.

STICKY PREDICAMENT

In March 2007, police in Magdeburg, Germany, rescued a 91-year-old man who slipped while resurfacing his roof and became glued to it by the tar.

BLIND POLICE

Many criminal investigations are solved in Belgium thanks to a blind police unit. The pioneering six-member unit specializes in transcribing and analyzing wiretap recordings and, because they have been trained to identify voices and background sounds, they often pick up evidence that sighted detectives have missed.

SILVER BEETLE

Art car enthusiast William Burge from Houston, Texas, has designed a vehicle with a gargoyle theme. Called "Phantoms," it is based on a 1968 Volkswagen Beetle and proved a scary sight at an automobile fair in Essen, Germany, in December 2007.

To celebrate the release of "The Simpsons Movie" on DVD, Donut King in Sydney, Australia, created a mighty donut that weighed nearly 4 tons—the equivalent of two rhinoceroses. Consisting of more than 90,000 individual donuts, half a ton of pink icing, and 66 lb (30 kg) of sprinkles, it measured 20 ft (6 m) in diameter and took 40 people more than nine hours to build.

MONSTER DONUT

KRYSTAL KING!

Joey Chestnut, 23, of San Jose, California, ate 103 Krystal burgers in just eight minutes at the Krystal Square Off IV World Hamburger Eating Championship at Chattanooga, Tennessee, in October 2007—that works out to 13 burgers per minute or one burger every 4.6 seconds!

After his incredible eating feat, Joey Chestnut said all he wanted to do was take a nap and digest his food.

Chestnut's achievement in becoming the first person to break the seemingly inconceivable 100-Krystal-burgers-in-eight-minutes barrier confirmed his position as the world's leading competitive eater.

FAVORITE JERSEY

David Witthoft, a young Green Bay Packers' football fan from Ridgefield, Connecticut, was so excited by his 2003 Christmas gift—a Packers' jersey with Brett Favre's No.4—that he wore it every day for four years. By the end of 2007, 11-year-old David had worn the jersey for more than 1,450 consecutive days.

SHOE SNIFFER

A man in Nagoya, Japan, was arrested in 2006 for stealing 5,000 pairs of shoes, which he took only to smell them.

FAILED CROSSING

In March 2007, a man tried to cross the fast-flowing Niagara River from Canada into the United States on an inflatable air mattress. Hearing the man's screams, guards at the Ontario Power Generation plant at Chippawa plucked him from the water as he was being swept toward Niagara Falls on a small ice floe while still clinging to the mattress.

MAIL TOWER

Artist Anne Cohen from Newcastle, England, turned a year's worth of unwanted junk mail into a garden sculpture. She put all the junk mail she received on a large metal spike outside her front door and by the end of 2007 the tower was more than 6 ft (1.8 m) tall.

BELATED GRADUATION

A Utah woman received her high school diploma in 2007—at age 94. Leah Moore Harris Fullmer missed her graduation ceremony from Provo High School in 1931 because of illness and did not pick up her diploma, but her son persuaded the school to trace her records and present it to her before her 95th birthday.

COUGHED BULLET

In October 2007, a month after he was shot in the mouth, Austin Askins of Liberty Lake, Washington, miraculously coughed up the bullet that surgeons previously had been unable to remove.

WIDE CHOICE

There were so many candidates in Bulgaria's 2007 local elections that the ballot papers were 6½ ft (2 m) long.

COMPLAINTS' CHOIR

A Finnish couple have put together a series of choirs that complain in four-part harmony about subjects ranging from bad dates to people who chew gum too loudly. Oliver Kochta-Kalleinen and Tellervo Kalleinen have started more than 20 complaints' choirs all over the world, from Melbourne, Australia, to Chicago, Illinois. In Birmingham, England, the choir sang about the country's expensive beer; in Helsinki, Finland, singers bemoaned boring dreams; and in Budapest, Hungary, choristers ranted about a neighbor practicing folk dancing in an upstairs apartment. Participants do not need to come from a musical background, but they must offer at least one complaint for possible inclusion in the performance.

CAROUSEL CONTEST

Four couples spent seven days on a rotating carousel in Xiamen, China, in an endurance contest to win a house. They had to stay on the fairground horses to eat, drink, and sleep—and were allowed to climb off only for toilet breaks. The contestants wore safety belts so that they did not fall off their horses while sleeping.

MOWER CHASE

A man accused of drunk driving tried to escape from the police on a lawn mower. The man was riding the mower near his home in Bunker Hill, West Virginia, when a sheriff's deputy pulled him over on suspicion of being drunk. The suspect attempted to speed away on the mower, but was easily outpaced by the deputy—on foot.

FOUND FRIEND

A vivid dream led a Canadian woman to a remote spot where she found a missing family friend. Jamie Lynn Cunningham of Gift Lake, Alberta, studied a sweater, a missing person's poster, and Native American Indian treaty card belonging to Michael Nahachick, who had not been seen for a month, and then dreamed Michael had fallen off a bridge at High Prairie, 25 mi (40 km) away. The next day she and fellow searchers found him, alive, at the exact spot under the bridge.

YELLOW DOOR

In 2007, Khumi Burton received a postcard sent from Poland that had been simply addressed to: Khumi, Yellow Door, Wilmslow, England.

37 SUSPECTS

When town Mayor Miguel Grima was found murdered in January 2007, police investigating the death declared all 37 residents of the village of Fago, Spain, as suspects in the case.

GOLF SPARK

In June 2007, a golfer in Reno, Nevada, struck a metal object with a golf swing and created a spark that ignited a wildfire, which destroyed 20 acres (8 ha) of land before finally dying out.

DRESS CODE

The Red Hat Society has more than 40,000 chapters in 30 countries around the world and has only two rules for its female members—they all must wear red hats and purple dresses.

BALLOON BART

Here are the Simpsons as you have never seen them before—made entirely out of balloons. They are the work of Washington State balloon artist Adam Lee, whose other creations include balloon likenesses of Jay Leno, Austin Powers, Bill Gates, Martha Stewart, and the Statue of Liberty.

SMASHING PUMPKINS

If you ever doubted that the pumpkin really is a squash fruit, the proof is at the Pumpkin Drop, a weird ritual that takes place each year before the Giant Pumpkin Weigh-off near Canby, Oregon. At 10 a.m. sharp, and watched by a crowd of around 4,000 admirers, a huge pumpkin (the 2007 specimen weighed 1,269 lb/575 kg) is loaded on to a crane and hoisted 100 ft (30 m) into the air above an old vehicle donated especially for the occasion. Once in position, the pumpkin is dropped from its great height onto the roof of the unoccupied van, crushing it to pieces.

POOL STOLEN
Thieves stole a 1,000-gal (4,550-l) hip-high, inflatable swimming pool from the home of Daisy Valdivia in Patterson, New Jersey—water and all!

UNEXPECTED RETURN
A man being discharged from the hospital ended up back inside after his mother hit him with her car when she went to collect him. Ron Carter was walking to meet his 84-year-old mother Lillian outside Elliot Hospital, New Hampshire, when she accidentally ran him over.

HAIRY EYE
Summitt, a dog living in Owensboro, Kentucky, has had hairs growing from the tissue of her right eye since she was a puppy.

CHICKEN RUN
Scared by a dog, a four-year-old Chinese boy let out such a loud scream that it caused a poultry stampede that killed more than 400 chickens.

ARMED SHRUBBERY
A bank in Manchester, New Hampshire, was robbed in 2007 by a man disguised as a tree. He walked in with leaves and branches duct-taped to his head and body and demanded money.

BALLOON JOURNEY
In September 2007, four-year-old Alice Maines of Manchester, England, released a balloon with a note attached—and 6,000 mi (9,660 km) and six weeks later it was recovered by 13-year-old Xie Yu Fei in Guangzhou, China.

COMPLIMENT MACHINE
Artist Tom Greaves built a machine that dispensed random compliments to passersby on 14th Street, Washington, D.C., in 2007. Placed on a street corner, the machine contained 150 pre-recorded compliments, ranging from "nice eyes" to "positive energy."

FISH ATTACK
Fisherman Josh Landin was taken to a hospital in Melbourne, Florida, after a 57-lb (26-kg) king mackerel jumped into his boat, knocked him over, and bit him on the leg.

LEG HAIR
Medical student Wes Pemberton from Tyler, Texas, has a leg hair that is 5 in (13 cm) long. He spotted the stray strand growing from his left thigh in the summer of 2007 and began nurturing it by washing it daily with shampoo and conditioner.

SHOT BY DOG
A hunter in Iowa was shot in the leg by his own dog. James Harris of Tama was hunting pheasants in October 2007 when his dog stepped on his shotgun and tripped the trigger, dispatching more than 100 pellets into his master's calf.

CHEESE LOVER
Owing to a food phobia, Dave Nunley from Cambridgeshire, England, has eaten nothing but cheese for more than 25 years. He has never had a hot meal in his life—not even melted cheese—and survives by eating 238 lb (108 kg) of grated mild cheddar every year.

SLIM FIT
Artez Kenyetta Knox escaped jail in Gary, Indiana, by taking his clothes off and amazingly squeezing through the cell door's food-tray slot.

FOWL SENTENCE
Instead of giving three prisoners a 30-day jail sentence each, Municipal Judge Michael Cicconetti ordered them to stand outside the courthouse in Painesville, Ohio, wearing chicken suits.

NAME CHANGE
Scott Wiese of Forsyth, Illinois, bet that if his favorite team, the Chicago Bears, lost the Super Bowl in 2007, he would change his name to that of the opposing team's quarterback. The Bears did lose to the Indianapolis Colts and so Wiese filed to have his name legally changed to the Colts' quarterback—Peyton Manning.

GREEN SHEEP
A flock of 250 sheep in a Romanian village suddenly turned green overnight. Veterinarians discovered that the color change had been caused by a limestone solution that shepherd Cristinel Florea had given to the animals in order to cure a skin disease.

SILENT WORLD
In 2007, a boy who had taken a vow of silence when he was three years old finally spoke again for the first time in ten years. Ben Grocock of Cornwall, England, was so terrified at the prospect of a tonsil operation that he threatened never to speak again if it went ahead. True to his word, once his tonsils had been removed, he relied mainly on written notes and hand signals to communicate over the following decade.

LOTTO LUCK
The odds of winning the New York Lotto jackpot once are 22.5 million to one, but Adeline and Eugene Angelo have done it twice. In 1996, they won $2.5 million after splitting a $10 jackpot with three others, and then in 2007, with luck on their side, they picked up a $5-million prize.

HUMAN ASHTRAY
In 2007, a gravedigger in Fitchburg, Massachusetts, was charged with stealing human body parts—including a skull and a thigh bone—from a broken casket at a cemetery and taking them home to make an ashtray.

COSTLY ERROR
Instead of sending out just one winning ticket, a marketing company in Roswell, New Mexico, mistakenly dispatched 50,000 scratch-off tickets that declared the ticket holder the winner of the $1,000 grand prize. The company blamed a typographical error.

JUDGMENT DAY
Immediately after being sentenced to five years in prison for theft, David Kite of Belleville, Illinois, was married in a civil wedding ceremony—by the same judge that presided over his criminal trial.

27

Ripley's Believe It or Not!®

ONE SIZE FITS ALL!

Shazneen's sketch of the dress. As the building faces the sea, the weather was very windy and Shazneen had to hire three men to hold the fabric in place so that it could be stitched.

In order to make the dress, Shazneen had to transport her sewing machine up to the terrace of the building. There she had to construct a tent to protect herself from the fierce heat.

The dress was supported by thin scaffolding, which took workers more than 12 hours to erect and fit securely behind the garment.

Shazneen's dress was unveiled on a giant hanger—made of metal pipes—from the front of the Sunder Mashal building on Mumbai's Marine Drive.

Indian designer Shazneen Chiniwala made a dress that was an incredible 70 ft (21 m) long for a fashion week in Mumbai in March 2007—that's big enough to fit more than a dozen ordinary-sized women. It took the 26-year-old two months to finish the dress, which was made of plastic and colored jute.

SLEEP WASH

Mrs. Xu, of Wuhan City, China, regularly washes the family's clothes in the middle of the night—while she is still asleep. She has been sleepwalking for more than ten years and her husband has had to put locks on the door to stop her leaving the house and washing neighbors' clothes.

ACCURATE TIPSTER

Four days before the 1959 Kentucky Derby, psychic Spencer Thornton of Nashville, Tennessee, wrote his prediction for the first three horses to finish on a piece of paper. The paper was sealed, unread, in an envelope and placed in a vault of the Third National Bank. The vault could be unlocked only by a combination of three keys, kept by two vice-presidents and its custodian—and it was not until two days after the race that the three men opened the vault and the envelope to reveal that Thornton's prediction was 100 percent correct.

COMPULSORY GOLF

Xiamen University in Fujian, China, requires all its business, law, economics, and computer students to take golf lessons.

COW CRUSHER

A couple driving through Washington State on vacation to celebrate their first wedding anniversary miraculously survived after a cow weighing 600 lb (270 kg) fell off a cliff 200 ft (60 m) high and landed on their moving minivan. Charles and Linda Everson from Westland, Michigan, escaped unhurt by the incident, but their van was badly damaged and the windshield smashed. A shocked Mr. Everson said: "It was just bam—you just saw something come down and hit the hood!"

LOST IN TRANSLATION

After having what she thought was the word "mum" tattooed on her back in Chinese letters, 19-year-old Charlene Williams was shocked to find that her tattoo actually said "Friend from hell." The mother-of-one from Dorset, England, did not realize that Chinese letters change their meaning when joined together. She has since had the tattoo covered over with a new design.

HUGE HAIRBALL

A barber for more than 50 years, Henry Coffer of Charleston, Missouri, has been collecting customers' clippings and has turned them into a huge hairball weighing over 160 lb (73 kg).

NICE PROFIT

In 2005, Ed Lee of Merrimack, New Hampshire, sold a 1913 nickel coin for $4.15 million—that's 83 million times its original value!

BURGER MISSION

Jay Barr of Cape Coral, Florida, makes an hour-long, 150-mi (240-km) flight to Kissimmee, Florida, ten times a year—just to buy hamburgers. He buys them in packs of 24 from the nearest Krystal fast-food restaurant. The Krystal company was so impressed by Mr. Barr's devotion to their burgers that it unveiled a hamburger box and drink cup with Barr's face and an airplane printed on them.

DREAM WEDDING

David Brown of London, England, sent a text message to a phone number that came to him in a dream. The woman on the other end of the text was Michelle Kitson and, intrigued, she responded. The two of them married five years later.

BIRTHDAY REMINDER

Vanda Jones of Penygroes, Wales, had the birthdays of all her five children tattooed on her arm so that she could be sure never to forget them.

ANCIENT FRUIT

In 2007, a museum in Staffordshire, England, displayed a 116-year-old orange. The blackened, dried-up fruit came from the lunchbox of coal miner Joseph Roberts, who was fatally injured in an underground explosion in 1891—sadly, before he got to eat his orange.

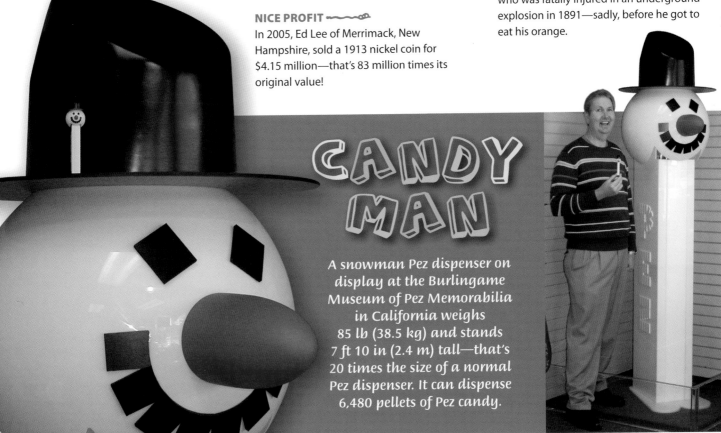

CANDY MAN

A snowman Pez dispenser on display at the Burlingame Museum of Pez Memorabilia in California weighs 85 lb (38.5 kg) and stands 7 ft 10 in (2.4 m) tall—that's 20 times the size of a normal Pez dispenser. It can dispense 6,480 pellets of Pez candy.

FLOATING PUB

A ship sailed 15,000 mi (24,000 km) from New Zealand to England in 2007 carrying an entire pub. When Tim Ellingham moved to London he asked friends back in New Zealand to send him his favorite Speights beer. Hearing of his predicament, the brewery decided to build a pub, fill it with beer, and ship it to the U.K. on board a cargo vessel. The pub was built in two 40-ft (12-m) containers joined together and came complete with bar, lounge, air conditioning, and plasma TV.

CHINESE VAMPIRE

Li Man-Yiu of Hong Kong was arrested in September 2007 for stealing and drinking two vials of blood from a hospital laboratory.

KIDNEY DONOR

Jamie Howard knocked on Paul Sucher's door at Twin Falls, Idaho, hoping to sell him a vacuum cleaner, but ended up giving him a kidney instead. Traveling salesman Howard learned that Sucher could not afford a new vacuum cleaner because of kidney failure three years earlier and so when he discovered that they were the same blood type, he generously offered to become Sucher's donor.

LATE ARRIVAL

A postcard sent by a Japanese soldier from Burma in 1943 finally reached its destination 64 years later. The card arrived at Shizuo Nagano's home in Japan's southwestern state of Kochi via Nagasaki, Arizona, and Hawaii.

UNWANTED GIFT

Owing to a postal mix-up, Frank and Ludivine Larmande of Cascade, Michigan, accidentally received a preserved human liver and part of a head in the mail, both intended for a lab.

THIRD EAR

Australian Stelios Arcadiou—known as Stelarc—has had an extra ear grafted onto his left arm... all in the name of art. He plans to install a microphone into the extra ear, which is made of human cartilage, and connect it to the Internet so that people everywhere can hear the sounds it picks up.

MOTORCYCLING FROG

When it comes to talented pets, Oui the frog must be unique—because she can ride a miniature motorcycle and predict winning lottery numbers! The frog's owner, Tongsai Bamnungthai of Pattaya, Thailand, says local people used to come and read Oui's stomach to determine lucky numbers, and that Oui loves to play with children's toys and to pose for photographs.

STAYING PUT

A 59-year-old prisoner in Brandenburg, Germany, has repeatedly been offered early release since 1992—but he refuses to leave the penitentiary that has become his home. The man was given life imprisonment for murder in 1972 and under German law prisoners are not obliged to leave jail before their sentences have been completed.

HALF SHARE

To protest against his pending divorce, a 43-year-old man in Sonneberg, Germany, cut his house in half with a chainsaw and then used a forklift truck to take his half away.

SPACE IMAGES

Natalie Meilinger of Chicago, Illinois, found that instead of turning on the TV for the latest news on NASA's 2007 *Atlantis* space shuttle, all she had to do was switch on her baby's monitor. The monitor mysteriously picked up black-and-white video images from inside the shuttle.

MEMORY LOSS

British musician Clive Wearing cannot remember anything from 1985 to the present day owing to a brain infection, but he can remember everything prior to 1985.

CRASH PREMONITION

After suffering nightmares on ten successive nights about an impending passenger-plane crash involving an American Airlines DC-10, David Booth, a 23-year-old office manager from Cincinnati, Ohio, reported his fears to the relevant authorities on May 22, 1979. Three days later, an American Airlines DC-10 crashed at Chicago's O'Hare International Airport, killing 273 people.

GHOST SHIP

In April 2007, a yacht was found off the coast of Australia with all of its emergency equipment intact and dinner on the table—but its three-member crew had disappeared without a trace.

EXPLODING TOADS

The toad population of Hamburg, Germany, was decimated in 2005 when several thousand of the creatures mysteriously exploded, sending entrails and body parts over a wide area. Witnesses said the toads swelled up to three-and-a-half times their normal size before suddenly exploding.

DEAD FISH

Millions of anchovies mysteriously washed ashore near Colunga, Spain, in September 2006, leaving the beach covered with three tons of dead fish.

DRUNK RIDER

A German man rode his horse into the foyer of a bank to sleep off his hangover. Wolfgang Heinrich of Wiesenberg had been riding his horse, Sammy, when he stopped to have a few drinks. Too drunk to ride home, he used his bank card to open up a nearby bank foyer and spent the night there with Sammy.

DARING JUGGLER

Nathan Zorchak, an American entertainer based in Brighton, England, can not only juggle scythes and bowling balls, but also three live chainsaws.

SWEET-TOOTHED BEAR

A man returned to his van in Vernon Township, New Jersey, in 2007 to find that it had been raided by a bear that had moved it 40 ft (12 m) down the street. Police believe the bear broke in to the van through the window because he could smell the Halloween candy. As he reached for the candy, the bear is thought to have dislodged the parking brake, causing the vehicle to roll down the hill.

SELF-PORTRAITS

In May 2007, U.S. artist Karl Baden exhibited contact prints of the 7,305 photographs he had taken of himself—that's one photograph a day every day since February 23, 1987. The only day he missed in that 20-year period was October 15, 1991, when he was late for a class he was teaching at Rhode Island School of Design. Baden had planned to do the picture afterward but then forgot.

GATOR WRESTLING

For $100 you can buy a day's tuition in... alligator wrestling. Colorado Gators, near Alamosa, is an alligator farm where people can learn to wrestle reptiles up to 11 ft (3.4 m) long and weighing 600 lb (270 kg). The key to success is a stealthy approach, although even experienced wrestler Jay Young gets bitten at least once a year. "These are not mild-mannered animals," he says, "and if they're breathing, they're in a bad mood."

ROADKILL TOYS

A British soft toy company has launched a range of animal characters that have all been run over. Twitch the roadkill raccoon has his tongue hanging out, one eyeball smashed in, and comes with a zipper that spills his innards and an opaque plastic body bag to keep out maggots. A label attached to his toe gives details of his grisly death. Other roadkill victims include Splodge the hedgehog and Pop the weasel.

LIZARD SMUGGLER

In 2007, a man named Jereme James, from Los Angeles, California, was accused of smuggling three rare iguana lizards into the United States—by hiding them inside his prosthetic leg. He allegedly hollowed out a secret compartment inside his false leg and used it to smuggle banded iguanas from Fiji. According to the prosecution, James had previously admitted to selling the rare lizards for up to $10,000 each.

MULE MISSION

In 2007, Rod Maday of Boy River, Minnesota, rode his four-year-old mule, named Henry, 1,500 mi (2,415 km) to Gilette, Wyoming, in search of work. Maday, who had lost his driver's license ten years previously, rode up to 70 mi (112 km) a day and made the six-week trek in full cowboy gear.

GNOM-ADIC

The police station at Springfield, Oregon, was overrun by lawn gnomes in 2007. The 75 plastic and porcelain ornaments were recovered by officers from the front lawn of a house where they had been placed as a prank after being stolen from gardens around the town.

SHEEP ACCOMMODATION

A man in Apex, North Carolina, shared his house with 80 sheep. David Watts lived upstairs while the flock, which he considered to be pets, lived downstairs. He sometimes took selected sheep for walks on a leash around the neighborhood.

THE LAW IS AN ASS

The chief witness in a 2007 court case in Dallas, Texas, was a donkey. Buddy was led into the courtroom to help resolve a dispute between two neighbors.

KITTY COPS

Thai police chiefs have come up with a new way to discipline officers who break rules—making them wear a Hello Kitty armband. The bright pink armband has a Hello Kitty motif and two embroidered hearts and is designed to shame the wearer.

TREES MARRIED

Two trees that grew around each other in West Bengal, India, were married by villagers in 2006 in a bid to keep evil spirits at bay. More than 250 people attended the ceremony, where priests chanted hymns and decorated the conjoined trees with colorful garments.

FALLING CAT

A woman from Chongqing, China, was taken to a hospital in 2007 after being knocked out by a cat falling from a high-rise apartment building. The tumbling cat hit Tang Meirong on the head as she walked along a footpath. Tang survived her ordeal but, sadly, the cat had used up its ninth life and was pronounced dead at the scene.

ALARM MIMIC

A pet parrot that loves to imitate sounds helped save a Muncie, Indiana, family from a house fire in 2007—by mimicking a smoke alarm. As flames ripped through their home, Shannon Conwell and his son slept through the real smoke alarm but were woken by Peanut the parrot's squawking imitation of it.

CROC FROCK

A woman tried to cross the border between Egypt and Gaza with three crocodiles strapped to her waist. The 20-in-long (50-cm) crocodiles had their jaws tied shut with string and were concealed under a loose robe, but the woman's "strangely fat" appearance alerted Palestinian guards at the crossing.

HEAVY HEDGEHOG

A hedgehog found in Surrey, England, weighed four times the size of a normal hedgehog. George tipped the scales at a whopping 4 lb 14 oz (2.2 kg) and was so fat that he had to be placed on a crash diet by an animal center.

Boar Island

A 250-lb (115-kg) wild boar called Babe lives a life of luxury on his own private island in the Bahamas. Babe lives on the island with its only two human inhabitants, Luke Abbott and Mona Wiethuchter, who feed him hot dogs, apples, and pasta and watch him stroll along the beach or go for a swim. For further relaxation, he enjoys a beer—but he has only one a day because with any more he can become a bit boisterous.

Index

Page numbers in *italics* refer to illustrations

ACKNOWLEDGMENTS

COVER (t/r) www.coloradogators.com, (b/r)Adam Lee www.adamlee.net; 6–7 Angie & Jimmy Taylor; 8 Peter Lawson/Rex Features; 9 (t/l, t/r) Steven R Kutcher, (l, b) AP/PA Photos; 10 Reuters/Lucas Jackson; 11 KNS News; 12 Daimler AG; 13 ChinaFotoPress/Photocome/PA Photos; 14 SWNS.com; 15 AP/PA Photos; 16 (t/l) David George Gordon, (c) ChinaFotoPress/Photocome/PA Photos, (r) Reuters/Staff Photographer; 17 (t) Tang Chhin Sothy/AFP/Getty Images, (b) Jorge Sanchez/AFP/Getty Images; 20 (c) SWNS.com; 21 Reuters/Victor Kintanar; 22 Martin Meissner/AP/PA Photos; 23 Newspix/Rex Features; 24 The Krystal Company; 25 Adam Lee www.adamlee.net; 26–27 Your Country Escape, LLC; 29 Robert George Clegg Industries; 30 Reuters/Sukree Sukplang; 31 (t) Roger Bamber/Rex Features, (b) www.coloradogators.com; 32 (t) Rex Features, (b) Solent News/Rex Features; 33 Gary Roberts/Rex Features

Key: t = top, b = bottom, c = center, l = left, r = right, sp = single page, dp = double page

All other photos are from Ripley Entertainment Inc.
Every attempt has been made to acknowledge correctly and contact copyright holders and we apologize in advance for any unintentional errors or omissions, which will be corrected in future editions.